SCIENCE ENCYCLOPEDIA

ENERGY AND EVOLUTION

Om
KIDZ

An imprint of Om Books International

Contents

Potential Energy 4

Kinetic Energy 5

Electrical Energy 6

Renewable Energy 7

Nuclear Energy 8

Solar Energy 9

Food and Chemical Energy 10

Fuel Cells 11

Energy Technology 12

Conversion of Energy 13

Mass-Energy Equivalence 14

Law of Conservation of Energy 15

International Energy Law 16

Evolution of Birds 18

Mechanism of Evolution 19

Variation 20

Food Chain 21

Human Evolution 22

Extinction of Species 24

Know Your Gene 26

Mutation 27

The Birth of New Species 28

Genetics 30

Cloning 32

ENERGY

Energy is simply the capacity to perform a task.
To accomplish any task, be it lifting a suitcase, rotating
a fan or heating a bucket of water, a body/machine
requires a certain amount of energy. Energy can exist
in many forms; potential, kinetic, thermal, electrical,
nuclear and so on. These forms of energy can be
converted from one form to another (although with
varying degrees of efficiency, depending on the particular
pair), but energy can never be destroyed. The sum total
of energy in the universe or in an isolated body is always
constant, which is a property called the conservation of energy.

Potential Energy

Potential energy is the energy that a body has because of its position or configuration in a force field. Depending on the kind of force field, potential energy is of several types: electrical, gravitational, nuclear, etc. These fields must necessarily be conservative, that is, an energy type that is conserved and recoverable during any work done by this force alone.

Elastic potential energy

Elastic potential energy is the second form of potential energy. It refers to the energy that is stored in elastic materials as a result of their stretching or compressing. It can be stored in rubber bands, bungee cords, trampolines, springs and an arrow drawn into a bow among others. The amount of elastic potential energy stored in such a device is related to the amount of stretch of the device, that is, the more the stretch, the more the stored energy. Springs are an excellent example of a device that can store elastic potential energy due to either compression or stretching.

Gravitational potential energy

Gravitational potential energy is the energy which is stored in an object because of its vertical position or height. The energy is stored due to Earth's gravitational attraction on an object. The gravitational potential energy of the massive ball of a demolition machine depends on two variables: the mass of the ball and the height to which it is raised. There is a direct relation between the gravitational potential energy and the mass of an object. The more massive the object, the greater the gravitational potential energy. Furthermore, there is a direct connection between gravitational potential energy and the height of an object. Similarly, the higher an object is elevated, the greater is the gravitational potential energy.

An object at a height has potential energy as gravity is acting on it and can cause the object to fall.

Latent energy

Potential energy represents the latent energy in a system. It can be converted into an active energy or motion when required, in relation with the conservation of energy, so that the energy is retained. For example, if we release a ball from a height of 15 m above the ground, it steadily loses its potential energy but gains kinetic energy as it comes down.

Kinetic Energy

Kinetic energy is the energy that a body possesses by virtue of its motion; a body at rest has zero kinetic energy. Mathematically, it is defined as half the product of the mass and the square of its velocity. Therefore, a body with a mass of 2 kg moving at a speed of 3 m/s has kinetic energy that is equal to 9 joule.

Change in kinetic energy

The mechanical work performed on a body is entirely revealed by the change in its kinetic energy. The type of motion involved may be translational (motion along a path from one place to another), rotational on an axis, vibrational or any combination of motions. The total kinetic energy is the sum of the kinetic energies associated with each kind of motion.

Forms of kinetic energy

Kinetic energy comes in different forms. Energy due to vibrational motion is called vibrational energy. Rotational energy is the energy due to rotational motion, while the energy due to motion from one location to another is called transitional energy. The translational kinetic energy that an object possesses depends upon two variables namely the mass and speed of an object.

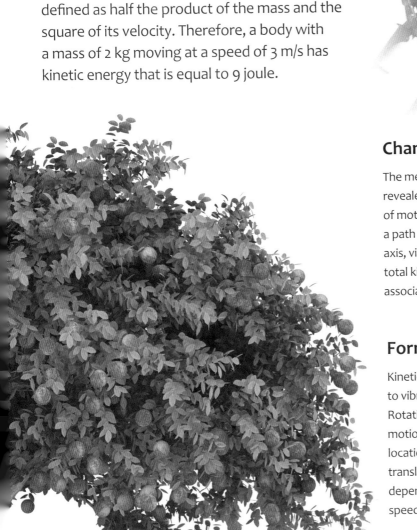

A falling object has kinetic energy as it is in motion.

Electrical Energy

Electrical energy is a kind of kinetic energy that is formed because of the movement of electric charges. It is a form of kinetic energy because the electric charges are continuously in motion. The speed of electric charge determines the amount of electrical energy.

Power grid supplies electricity everywhere.

Uses of electrical energy

By virtue of the ease with which it can be transported from one place to another, or converted into other forms of energy, electrical energy holds enormous importance in the fields of technology and engineering. For lighting, operation of electronic equipment, automotive engines, entertainment applications and a variety of other uses, electric energy has no rival. Electric power is produced by generators, which work on the induction principle proposed by the legendary English experimental physicist Michael Faraday in 1831. The power is usually supplied to homes and businesses by the means of a power grid.

Hydroelectric power plant.

Sources of electrical energy

Traditionally, there have been two sources of electricity generation – hydro and thermal. Hydroelectricity involves creating massive dams across rivers and harnessing the kinetic energy of the flowing river water to run the electric generator and generate power. The thermal alternative basically depends on burning fossil fuels like coal or petroleum to produce heat that runs the electric generator. Nowadays, due to concerns over the environmental cost of thermal power plants in particular, that supply a lion's share of worldwide electricity demand, other sources of electricity generation are also coming into vogue, such as nuclear energy, solar plants, wind turbines and geothermal power stations.

Renewable Energy

Renewable energy is also known as alternative energy. It is made from sources of energy that are infinite or replenishable. Renewable energy makes use of the energies of the Sun, wind, tides, flowing water and so on.

The need for renewable energy

At the beginning of the twenty first century, fossil fuels contributed to approximately 80 per cent of the worldwide power demand. However, burning fossil fuels has a grave environmental impact as the by-products of the combustion reaction wreak havoc on Earth's weather patterns, causing global warming and respiratory diseases in animals and human beings. Also, these fossil fuels are a finite and fast-depleting resource. They have been formed by long-term decomposition of organic matter and cannot be created at will. The world's oil deposits are estimated to run dry by the middle of this century.

FUN FACT

The warmest years recorded have been the past 10–12 years.

82 per cent of glaciers in Glacier National Park, Montana, have disappeared.

Types of renewable energy

To counter this problem, we have resorted to using resources that are not so finite, like the Sun (solar energy), wind (wind energy), hot springs and geysers (geothermal energy), tides (tidal energy) and rivers (hydroelectricity). However, there are a lot of problems associated with trying to utilise these forces of nature for our energy needs, all of which revolve around the unpredictability of these sources. If the Sun is blocked out by clouds, solar power is unfeasible. If winds are negligible, wind turbines become useless. Hot springs are too rare. Despite these hurdles and the need to optimise these technologies for maximum yield, these resources hold the promise of a cleaner future for us all.

Windmills and solar panels; sources of renewable energy.

Nuclear Energy

Nuclear energy can be harvested, at least in theory, from two types of reactions – nuclear fission and nuclear fusion. In fission, a large nucleus is bombarded with a much smaller particle to break it into two smaller nuclei. The process is accompanied by a large amount of energy. In nuclear fusion, two small atoms combine to form a larger atom, like helium, with the release of enormous amounts of energy.

Uses of nuclear energy

Both fission and fusion have been used in weapons of mass destruction. Scientists have only been able to extract energy in a controlled manner from fission. Although fusion is theoretically a far more productive and exciting source of energy, it is difficult to attain because of the high temperatures (up to 6 times the temperature at the centre of the Sun). Also, because it is difficult to confine the reaction, it continues by itself.

Nuclear explosion.

Problems with nuclear energy

While nuclear fission is used as a source of energy even now, there are certain problems associated with it – mainly due to the highly toxic, radioactive nature of the waste produced in a fission reactor. There are almost no suitable ways to safely dispose of this waste and they cause severe environmental degradation, and can cause a number of diseases in animals and humans who are within range of the radiation emitted by these wastes. Nuclear energy still remains a technology of the future.

Radiation supervisor checks the level of radioactive radiation in the danger zone.

Solar Energy

Solar energy is one of the most promising, effective and cleanest renewable energy alternatives currently available to humankind. It is rapidly becoming popular across the world. Sunlight is the largest source of energy received by Earth – despite the diffusion of the light caused by atmosphere, the light that is incident on Earth's surface is still more than enough to satisfy worldwide energy demands.

Uses of solar energy

Solar energy is utilised in two ways – to produce heat or to generate electricity. Solar thermal energy has been used to heat water, for space heating, space cooling and to process heat generation. Electricity generation is mainly done through solar cells or photovoltaic cells. In such cells, a small electric voltage is generated when light falls upon the junction between a metal and a semiconductor (such as silicon) or the junction between two different semiconductors. Solar energy is also used to drive chemical reactions to produce what is known as solar fuel.

Solar heater.

Disadvantages of solar energy

While solar energy is hugely promising, it has two major disadvantages. One – it is still costly and inefficient as most photovoltaic cells only have approximately 15–20 per cent conversion efficiency. Two – places with less sunlight or cloudy climates cannot effectively use solar energy.

Solar energy is used today, mostly in low-power, small scale applications, but this is bound to change in the future.

Solar cooking oven.

FUN FACT

If we were to use all the solar energy that Earth receives every year, we would be able to create energy that will be 8000 times the total world energy consumption.

Food and Chemical Energy

In biology, one thing that unites all living organisms, from the smallest amoeba to the largest blue whales, is their need for energy. In green plants, this energy is provided by the Sun. In animals, this energy is provided by consumption of plants or other animals. This is called an energy or food chain.

Energy sources

More complicated living organisms obtain their energy from a wide variety of nutrient groups, such as fats, carbohydrates, proteins and a few other chemicals. In humans, for example, these nutrients are simplified inside the body by the digestive system (using various enzymes) into a more manageable form like glucose and are later converted by the respiratory system into ATP in the presence of oxygen. The energy of food is generally measured in terms of the oxidative energy of food particles (using a bomb calorimeter and making corrections for the efficiency of digestion and absorption) and the unit used is a kilocalorie. This system was pioneered in the late nineteenth century by American chemist Wilbur Atwater and this method of measuring food energy is called the Atwater system.

Various sources of nutrition.

Energy in plants

Sunlight provides the thrust for photosynthesis reaction, where water, carbon dioxide and certain other minerals like potassium and phosphorous are converted with the help of sunlight (and the green chemical chlorophyll acting as a catalyst) to produce adenosine triphosphate, which is a sort of energy currency in living organisms. It can be utilised as and when necessary, through cellular respiration. Plants being the only living organisms capable of creating energy from the sun, the rest of the living organisms have to depend upon them for their energy requirements. Hence, plants alone are the energy providers for all the organisms on Earth.

Fuel Cells

A fuel cell is a class of devices where fuel is converted directly into energy by means of electrochemical reactions. The difference that these cells have in comparison to normal batteries is that while the batteries start off with a fixed amount of fuel material and oxidants that are slowly depleted to zero with use, the fuel material and oxygen in a fuel cell are constantly supplied, similar to how a DC generator system works.

Types of fuel cells

A fuel cell may be considered as a transducer that converts chemical energy to electrical energy. The primary fuels currently used are hydrogen, reformed natural gas (methane CH_4 transformed into hydrogen-rich gas) and methanol (CH_3OH). Depending on the kind of electrolyte used, these cells are classified into three categories: (i) alkaline fuel cells that use an aqueous solution of sodium or potassium hydroxide; (ii) phosphoric acid cells that use orthophosphoric acid (H_3PO_4) and (iii) molten carbonate fuel cells that use molten potassium lithium carbonate.

Uses of fuel cells

Fuel cells have been widely used for a long time in space probes and satellites, and are now finding wide acceptance as an energy source in hospitals, schools, hotels and waste-treatment plants. They are used to derive energy from the methane produced by decomposing garbage and in automobile engine units.

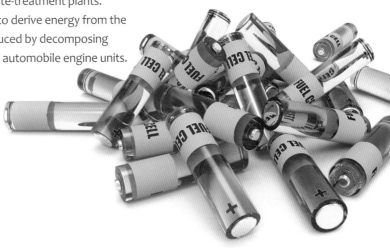

First certified fuel cell boat in the world.

Energy Technology

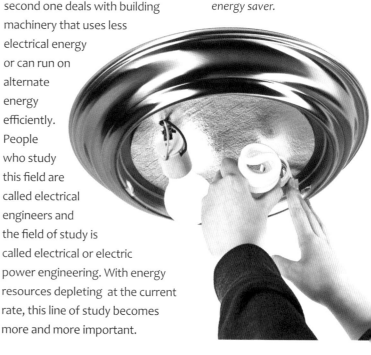

Energy technology is currently one of the most exciting fields of scientific research – its goal is to figure out ways of extracting energy from various fuel sources in a way that optimises its efficiency, minimises its costs and reduces its adverse impact on the environment, while also devising effective mechanisms for the transportation, distribution and storage of this energy. Energy is a scant resource, and has been the source of conflict and war many times in human history.

Reconstruction of the first electric battery.

Energy researchers

Humans have been experimenting with energy ever since the discovery of fire. There have been many legendary scientists and engineers who have made their mark in this field, for example, James Watt (inventor of the steam engine), Alessandro Volta (inventor of the battery), Frank Shuman (solar energy pioneer), Enrico Fermi (developed the first nuclear fission reactor based on the ideas of Szilard, Meitner, Strassmann and Hahn) and Nikola Tesla (pioneer of the alternating current). Moreover, as we head into the age of renewable energy and maybe even nuclear fusion, we will add to this list of luminaries with the next generation of energy researchers.

Steam engine.

Electric power engineering

Electric power has become an indispensable part of our daily life. It is hard to imagine a day without electricity, let alone a lifetime. Hence, there are scientists who are studying the sources of electricity and their uses. There are two parts to this study. The first one deals with efficient and economic ways of creating electricity, while the second one deals with building machinery that uses less electrical energy or can run on alternate energy efficiently. People who study this field are called electrical engineers and the field of study is called electrical or electric power engineering. With energy resources depleting at the current rate, this line of study becomes more and more important.

CFL bulb is an energy saver.

Conversion of Energy

Energy cannot be put to useful work in every form, so we usually convert it from one form to another as and when required. However, all these transformations are not equivalent, that is, energy transforms from one form to another with a range of efficiencies.

Laws of conversion

There are rigid limits imposed on the maximum efficiency with which work can be extracted from a given amount of energy, according to two theorems called the Carnot's theorem and the Second Law of Thermodynamics. The degree of efficiency of transformation between any two types of energy is determined by entropy considerations. Entropy is a measure of the randomness or disorder of a system and according to the Second Law of Thermodynamics, the entropy of the universe always increases in every natural physical process. Only those types of transformations are more likely to occur on a larger scale, where the overall disorder or entropy of a system increases; for example, electrical energy to heat.

Conversion of chemical energy to heat energy.

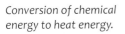

Daily application

Many events happen during our day when we don't realise that energy is being converted. When you eat and work out, the food energy is getting converted into kinetic and muscular energy. Energy gets converted every day all around us.

Transducers

Devices that transform one kind of energy into another are called transducers; for example, windmills that convert wind energy to mechanical energy for grinding grain and pumping water or the engine of a car that utilises the chemical energy of fossil fuels to generate kinetic energy.

Windmill is one of the best transducers.

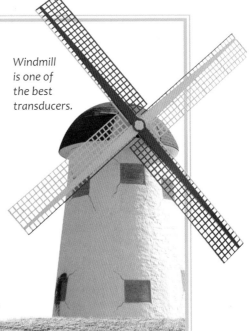

Mass-Energy Equivalence

In physics, the mass-energy equivalence is the concept that the energy content of a body also depends upon its mass rather than simply being a function of its speed, temperature or configuration in a force field. A ball with smaller mass will have less impact than one with more mass when dropped from the same height.

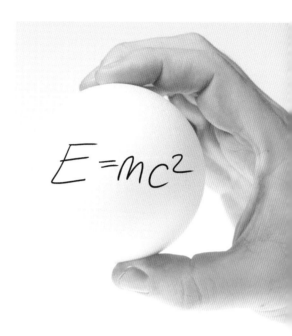

$$E = mc^2$$

Albert Einstein

The discovery

Albert Einstein put forward this radical re-imagining of energy in his 1905 paper, "Does the inertia of an object depend upon its energy content?", one of the three papers that he published that year (called the *Annus Mirabilis* or *Year of Miracles* papers) that led to a paradigm shift in modern physics and laid the foundation for three hugely important disciplines – relativity, quantum mechanics and statistical mechanics.

E = mc²

In this paper, Einstein showed that the energy content due to the mass of a body can be calculated by the formula $E = mc^2$, where c is the velocity of light, 3×108 m/s. Mass and energy are interchangeable and always connected by the same proportionality equation. This radically changes our idea of the universal conservation of energy, as now the quantity to be conserved is not just energy as we thought previously (let us call it E) but the sum total of E and the new-found mass energy. This is also the explanation of how, in nuclear bombs, a small amount of matter can produce so much energy, because a small part of the mass of the parent nuclei is converted to energy. Therefore, the statement of the conservation of energy postulate may now be defined as follows: The sum total of energy and mass in the universe or in any isolated physical system is constant.

A person using the same amount of energy to drive a small nail using a small hammer will have less impact than someone using the same energy to hit a spike with a sledgehammer.

Law of Conservation of Energy

The total energy of the universe or of an isolated physical system is always constant. This is the law of conservation of energy. It's one of the most important postulates and calculation tools in physics. According to Noether's theorem, the conservation of energy is a mathematical consequence of the fact that the laws of physics do not change with time; another foundational axiom.

Conversion of energy

In some cases, the notion of conservation of energy might seem counterintuitive. When we set a ball rolling on the ground, sooner or later, it will come to rest. Therefore, not only does it lose its kinetic energy, but its potential energy also shows no corresponding increase. However, the energy is only redirected elsewhere, as heat generated by the friction force exerted by the ground on the ball. To date, no exception to this law of energy conservation has been observed. If there was, everything we know about our universe would be brought into question.

Einstein's theory

Einstein postulated a now widely-accepted notion of how the mass of a body also contributes to its energy content, which is called the mass-energy equivalence. In general, if we're trying to be very precise in our definition, the sum total of energy and mass in the universe or in any isolated physical system is constant. This becomes the basis of the conservation of energy.

Conservation of energy can be understood by a simple example of a motorcycle, where the fuel acts as potential energy, which is consumed to impart kinetic energy to the motorcycle.

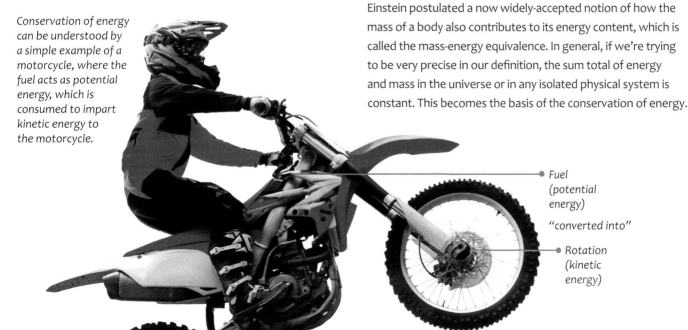

Fuel
(potential energy)

"converted into"

Rotation
(kinetic energy)

International Energy Law

The arena of international energy legislation is a complicated one. Every country has a different agency (and sometimes two or three), which controls the energy production and distribution within that country; for example, the Oil and Natural Gas Commission of India, the Australian Petroleum Production and Exploration Association, etc. These agencies also determine the overall energy policy.

Global energy consumption

Although most countries recognise the danger that rampant fossil fuel consumption poses to the environment, and the fact that fossil fuel deposits are fast depleting and will soon hit rock bottom, many countries, especially developing ones like China or India, often rely extensively on fossil fuels to power their high economic growth (as this form of energy is cheap and easy to generate). Nevertheless, almost all countries have some form of renewable energy programmes; some of them are highly successful.

FUN FACT

The total energy that the TV sets in the USA use when they are switched off can power a nuclear plant. This is because the TV sets use electricity to put them on standby so that they can instantly turn on when switched on.

Geothermal power plant in Iceland. Here, the thermal energy is generated and stored in Earth.

Alternative energy

Iceland's 80 per cent of energy needs are met by their own indigenous geothermal energy programme and more than 50 per cent of Germany's energy requirements are met by solar power. In addition, laws on carbon footprint and emission trading have made it cost-effective for most industries to use more renewable energy resources rather than oil or coal-based energy.

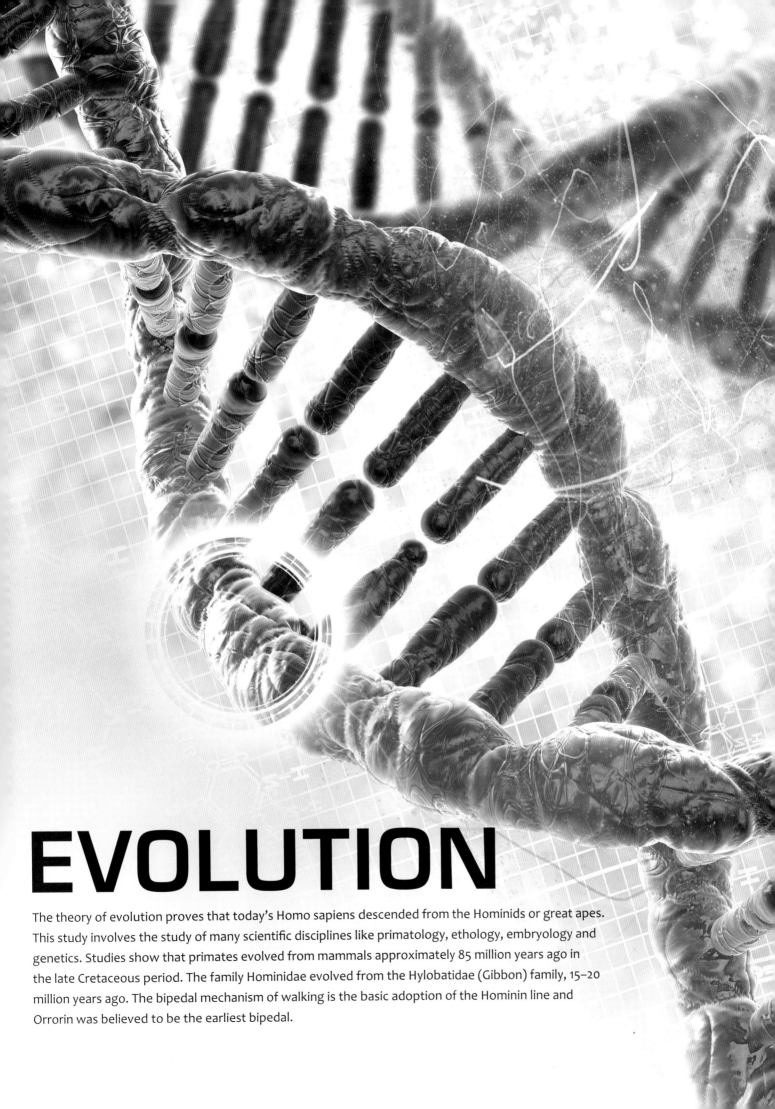

EVOLUTION

The theory of evolution proves that today's Homo sapiens descended from the Hominids or great apes. This study involves the study of many scientific disciplines like primatology, ethology, embryology and genetics. Studies show that primates evolved from mammals approximately 85 million years ago in the late Cretaceous period. The family Hominidae evolved from the Hylobatidae (Gibbon) family, 15–20 million years ago. The bipedal mechanism of walking is the basic adoption of the Hominin line and Orrorin was believed to be the earliest bipedal.

Evolution of Birds

The evolution of birds began in the Jurassic period, the earliest birds being the torpedo dinosaurs named Paraves. Birds belong to the class Aves. Archaeopteryx lithographica was the earliest known bird. Aves are considered to be the descendants of the ancestors of a specific modern bird species, like the house sparrow or an Archaeopteryx or some species close to the Neornithes.

Evolution of birds from dinosaurs

The house sparrow could have the same ancestors as all the aves.

Even after so many years of research and study, the debate regarding the relationship between the dinosaur, Archaeopteryx and modern birds still continues. Evolution, as we know, is a process that takes years. However, bird species are presently approaching the point of extinction faster than any other species. The extinction of a species shows the permanent loss of a range of genes. As birds are considered to be evolved from theropod dinosaurs, some of their properties seem to have changed in the process. There is no evidence that the animals were evolving into birds, but various complex steps helped in this.

Archaeopteryx lithographica.

For example, Compsognathus was the first species to have feathers. Short, hair-like feathers developed, which provided them insulation and protection. It is not proved why they were of different colour and sizes.

Evolution of wings

3D rendering of a dinosaur with developed wings and joints.

Another point of study is the change in the digits of dinosaurs. The first theropod dinosaurs had hands with small digits and one long digit. Many scientists showed that this would lead to the evolution of birds. Slowly, these digits were lost through the species. The wrist bones, underlying the first and second digits became semi-circular, which allowed the hand to rotate sideways. This allowed the birds' wing joints to move in a way that could create a thrust for flight. In spite of this, birds classification and phylogenetic studies are still undeveloped and require a lot of research.

Model of Tarbosaurus Tyrannosaurid Theropod Dinosaur with hands at a theme park.

Mechanism of Evolution

There are many mechanisms according to scientists that showed how a completely new species evolved from the existing one. This occurred by changes in the genes through generations. The methods by which the changes occurred are natural selection, biased mutation, genetic drift, genetic hitchhiking and gene flow.

Genetic hichhiking

The genes that are present close to chromosomes are difficult to be separated; thus, they are wholly inherited as a combination. If one of the genes is dominant, then the other gene gets profited and becomes prominent in the population. This process is called genetic hichhiking.

Natural selection

It is the process in which only the organisms that are more fit for the environment survive and others don't. This is the main principle of the process of natural selection. An organism produces more number of progeny than the number that survives and only organisms with genes that are more fit for the environment survive.

Genetic drift

It is the process by which, in the absence of selective forces, the frequency of a particular gene either increases or decreases. This can result in the evolution of a completely new species.

Gene flow

It is the exchange of genes between two populations or species.

Biased mutation

This is the main criteria for the selection of genes by nature. Consider two genes, A and B, having the same fitness for the environment, but mutation prefers gene A more than gene B. Then, more and more organisms with gene A are produced. Naturally, the population with gene A will increase.

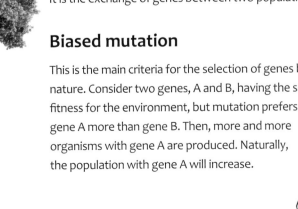

Long neck of a giraffe developed through adaptation.

Variation

An individual organism's physical appearance gets affected by both its genes and the effect of the surroundings. Changes in the physical appearance of organisms are caused due to differences in their genes. Variation occurs when a new allele substitutes an old one. Natural selection can be the cause of evolution if the offspring have a lot of genetic variation.

Inheritance

Before Mendel gave us the laws of genetics, inheritance was understood to be the main process. But if blending inheritance would have been true, genetic variance and natural selection would have to be completely discarded. The Hardy–Weinberg principle showed how variation occurred in a population. Selection, mutation, migration and genetic drift were the processes that cause variations in genes.

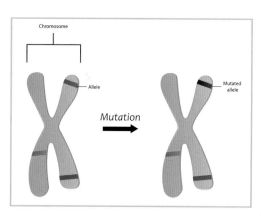

The process of mutation leading to changes in genes.

Variations in genes

Variation means mutations in genetic materials, reshuffling of genes and genetic migration between populations. Although there was a constant introduction of new variation by mutation and gene flow, the genetic structure of a species was identical in all individuals of a species. A little difference in the genetic structure could amount for a great change in the physical appearance of the species. For example, the human genes defer from chimpanzee genes by only 5 per cent!

Similarly, cat genes are different from human genes by only 10 per cent. The genes are present within every cell of the human body. Even the slightest change in genetic matter can rewrite the entire structure of the living being.

Food Chain

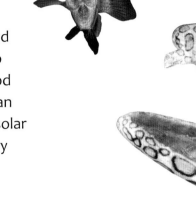

A food chain is the order of transfer of matter and energy in the form of food from one organism to another. Food chains intertwine locally into a food web because most organisms consume more than one type of animal or plant. Plants that convert solar energy to food by photosynthesis are the primary source of food.

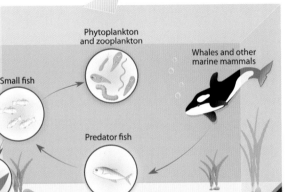

Solar energy

Marine food web.

Phytoplankton and zooplankton

Whales and other marine mammals

Small fish

Benthic organisms

Predator fish

Tiger attacks a deer that eats plants.

A real life food chain

Consider a grassland. There are various insects that live in it. One of them is a grasshopper that feeds on it. However, this grasshopper is then hunted by rats. Now, rats become prey for reptiles like snakes. So, snakes hunt the rats. Snakes are in turn hunted by predator birds like eagles. The food chain begins from grass and ends at the eagle. If the eagle were to die, it would be fed upon by the microorganisms in the soil, converting it into food for the plants. That is how the loop is closed.

Energy loss

As energy is lost at each step in the form of heat, chains do not normally encompass more than four or five tropic levels. People can increase the total food supply by removing one step in the food chain. Instead of consuming animals that eat plants, people eat plants directly. As the food chain is made shorter, the total amount of energy available to the final consumers is increased.

Food chain types

In a predator chain, a plant-eating animal is eaten by a flesh-eating animal. In a parasite chain, a smaller organism consumes a part of a larger host and may itself play host to even smaller organisms. In a saprophytic chain, microorganisms live on dead, organic matter.

Human Evolution

Human evolution is the process by which human beings developed on Earth from the now extinct primates. Zoologically speaking, humans are Homo sapiens, a culture-bearing, upright-walking species that live on the ground and first evolved in Africa between 100,000 and 200,000 years ago. We are now the only living members of what many zoologists refer to as the human tribe Hominini. However, there were many before us.

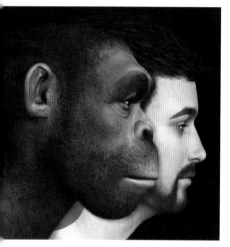

Current day humans and our predecessors have always shared Earth with other ape-like primates.

Historical evidence

The extensive process of change by which humans originated from ape-like ancestors is called human evolution. Scientific evidence shows that the physical and behavioural traits shared by all people originated from ape-like ancestors and evolved over a period of approximately six million years.

In addition, we and our predecessors have always shared Earth with other ape-like primates, from the modern-day gorilla to the long-extinct Dryopithecus. The extinct hominins are related to us and so are we and the apes (both living and extinct). This fact is accepted by anthropologists and biologists everywhere.

The skull of a Dryopithecus ancient ape.

Charles Darwin

The exact nature of our evolutionary relationships has been the subject of debate and investigation since the great British naturalist Charles Darwin published his monumental books *On the Origin of Species* (1859) and *The Descent of Man* (1871).

Darwin never claimed, as some of his Victorian contemporaries insisted he had, that "man descended from the apes", and modern scientists would view such a statement as a useless simplification—just as they would dismiss any popular notions that a certain extinct species is the "missing link" between man and the apes.

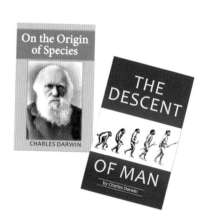

Charles Darwin's theory on the evolution of man.

The missing link

There is theoretically, however, a common ancestor between us and the apes that existed millions of years ago. This ancestral species does not constitute a "missing link" along a lineage but rather a node for divergence into separate lineages. This ancient primate has not been identified and may never be known with certainty, because fossil relationships are unclear even within the human lineage, which is more recent. In fact, the human "family tree" may be better described as a "family bush", within which it is impossible to connect a full chronological series of species, leading to Homo sapiens that experts can agree upon.

Creative representation of the prehistoric man.

Excavations and finds

Ancient human fossils and archeological remains give many vital clues about our evolution. These fossil remains include bones, tools and other evidences (such as footprints, evidence of hearths or butchery marks on animal bones). Ideally, the remains are buried and preserved naturally. They are usually found either on the surface due to exposure by rain, rivers and wind erosion or by digging the ground. Scientists learn about the physical appearance of the earlier humans and how it changed by studying fossilised bones. We can understand how these predecessors moved around, held tools and how the size of their brains changed over a long time by examining the bone size, shape and markings left on the bones by their muscles. We can understand how early humans made and used tools, and lived in their environments by studying archeological evidence. This helps us draw parallels to us as well as other species.

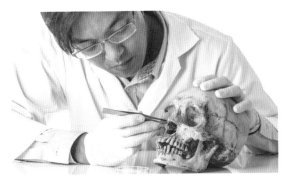

Scientist studying human fossil.

Extinction of Species

The causes of extinction were prehistorically dominated by natural Earth processes such as geological transformation of Earth's crust and major climatic oscillations, as well as species interactions. However, since the ascent of the modern man during the Holocene, the causes of extinction have been dominated by the activities of humans.

The Woolly Mammoth is an extinct species of elephant.

Extinct species

Thylacine, also known as the Tasmanian tiger, became extinct in 1936 as it was hunted to protect the sheep and small farm animals.

Quaggas became extinct in 1883 due to being hunted indiscriminately for their meat and leather.

Dodo birds became extinct around the 1670s. They were known to have been hunted by sailors on a large scale as they were so easy to catch. Also, the pets of these sailors had developed a taste for Dodo eggs.

Passenger Pigeons went extinct as recently as 1914. They were also hunted on a large scale for their meat.

FUN FACT

Sabre-toothed tiger evolved into the modern tiger by the process of migration.

Quagga is an extinct animal.

Causes of extinction

Darwin was the first to fully articulate the concepts of speciation and extinction as applied to natural succession, although he never used the terms evolution or extinction (1859). The primary cause of human-induced extinctions is simply the human overpopulation of planet Earth. The most important causal anthropogenic activities are habitat destruction, overexploitation, pollution and the introduction of alien species to an environment. Habitat destruction elements include conversion to agricultural land, deforestation, overgrazing and urbanisation. Within these activities, the process of habitat fragmentation is sometimes the hidden cause of major biodiversity loss. Overexploitation consists of intensive mineral and other geological resource extraction, overharvesting of wild flora and fauna (mainly for food), hunting or fishing, threatened fauna and killing of threatened fauna on a large scale for herbal or cultural extracts.

As per scientists, long lasting natural calamities are the major cause for extinction.

Extinct Dodo bird.

Natural mass extinction

Mass extinctions are periodic elevations in the extinction rate above the background level. Such extinctions are caused due to catastrophes. Approximately, over 95 per cent of all extinctions have occurred as background events with the rest consisting of catastrophic events. These events were geologically rapid, occurred worldwide, had a large number of species going extinct at the same time period and spread across all the world's ecosystems. The five major extinction events that have been recognised as the big 5 are as follows:

• The Ordovician event that happened 438 million years ago, when 100 families went extinct.

• The Devonian event, 360 million years ago, when 30 per cent of the families went extinct.

• The end Permian, 245 million years ago, the biggest extinction of all time when over 50 per cent of all families were lost.

• The late Triassic event when 35 per cent of the families died.

• The Cretaceous Tertiary (K-T) event, 65 million years ago, which ended the reign of the dinosaurs.

Human-driven extinction

The impact of pollution includes the build-up of toxic atmospheric substances, discharge of water pollutants into water reserves, chemical contamination of soils and noise pollution. Introduction of alien species is usually an unintended activity where seeds, stowaway fauna aboard ships and other viably reproducing biota are transported by humans to a new environment that has insufficient resident predators (or predators unfamiliar with and therefore naive to the new prey) to control the invading taxon or exotic predators. Here, the native fauna are often unable to recognise the invading organism as a threat and end up getting destroyed in large numbers.

Know Your Gene

The gene is a basic physical and functional unit of heredity that is transferred from an organism to its offspring and gives specific characteristics to the offspring. The word gene is taken from the Greek word genesis meaning "birth" or genos meaning "origin". The gene is a locatable region of genomic sequence, which is associated with regulatory regions, transcribed regions and other functional, sequence regions.

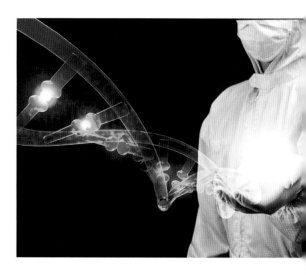

Women   *Men*

Female and male chromosomes.

Discovery of genes

Gregor Mendel worked from 1857 to 1864 on edible pea plants and found the evidence of a hereditary material. It was rediscovered by European scientists Hugo de Vries, Carl Correns and Erich von Tschermak. Charles Darwin gave the term gemmule for the unit of inheritance and that later came to be known as chromosome, coined by German biologist Wilhelm Hofmeister. The word gene was coined by Danish botanist Wilhelm Johannsen.

Function of gene

All organisms have genes related to their traits, from the eye colour to the many biochemical processes of life. The expression of genes encoded in DNA begins by the process of transcription of the gene into a messenger RNA. Genes also possess codons, which serve as words in the genetic language. Then, by the process of slicing and translation, a protein forms. The genes are translated from mRNA to protein. Genes act as instructions to make the molecules called proteins.

Gene expression

The process of producing a molecule of either RNA or protein that is biologically functional is called gene expression and the molecule that is produced at the end is called a gene product.

Genetic code

Genetic code is the rule by which the information in a gene is translated into a specific protein. The gene is a distinct arrangement of nucleotides, which determines the order of the monomers in a polypeptide. In human beings, most of the genes remain the same but less than one per cent are different because of which each person possesses his/her unique physical identity.

The transmission of genes enables the child to have the characteristics of its parents.

 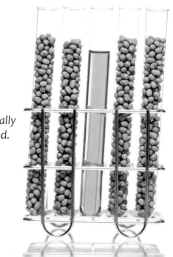

Mung bean is genetically modified.

Mutation

If we were to observe the natural places around us, we will find an enormous number of various beetles in different places. How can so many different organisms evolve having nearly, but not completely, the same genetic makeup? The answer is mutation. When a change takes place in the nucleotide in the genome of an organism, a sequence occurs. This is called mutation.

Few examples of different types of mutation of fruits and vegetables.

Exotic mutation in a pineapple making it look different from others.

Kiwi in apple is a modification concept.

Unusual mutation of carrot.

What is a mutation?

As nucleotides are the building blocks of DNA, their mutations cause changes in the phenotype of the organism. Mutations are also called errors in the genes. The frequency of the mutation is very low, around one in a hundred million bases. DNA polymerase plays an important role in carrying out mutations. There are some chemicals and also UV radiation that can cause mutations and are called as mutagenic substances.

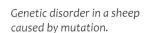

Types of mutations

Mutations can be classified on the basis of how much effect can they have on the structure, function, fitness or protein sequence, or on the basis of its inheritance ability. The main types of mutations are given below.

1. **Point mutations**
    It is the smallest mutation in which change occurs in only a base pair.
2. **Nonsynonymous mutations**.
    It is the mutation in which an amino acid sequence changes, thus forming a new protein.
3. **Synonymous mutations**.
    It is the mutation in which the change only occurs in the sequence that hold the code for the amino acids.

Genetic disorder in a sheep caused by mutation.

Effects of mutations

Mutation, however, is a very powerful tool as even a small mutation produces a large change in the phenotype. But if we consider the evolutionary aspect, it proves that a large number of mutations produce small effects. The mutations can be beneficial, harmful or neutral depending upon the context and location.

The Birth of a New Species

The term species is always being argued about. In biological terms, we can say that species is a group of organisms that interbreed and are reproductively separated from other organisms. Speciation is the word used for the process by which a completely new species evolves. In nature, the process of speciation occurs by four ways: allopatric, peripatric, parametric and sympatric.

Speciation

Speciation is the event of a lineage splitting that produces two or more separate species. It is usually difficult to estimate when speciation has occurred because it is a gradual process. If speciation has to occur, members of an ancestral species must be separated from each other. Thus, separating organisms into two populations results in two separate gene pools. These gene pools can be isolated through geographical or biological methods. Moreover, altered reproductive methods can isolate two populations of the same organisms.

Allopatric

This occurs when two populations of the same species separate geographically from one other. They adapt differently according to their environments. They face different mutations and genetic drifts, and become completely different species unable to reproduce with one other.

Peripatric

In this type of process of speciation, a small group of organisms gets separated from the rest of the population and slowly evolves into a different species than the main population, because of the genetic drift.

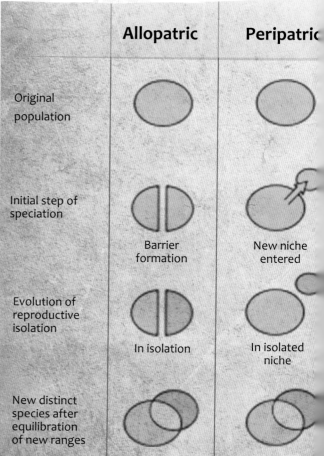

Dinosaurs extinct by natural selection.

	Allopatric	Peripatric
Original population		
Initial step of speciation	Barrier formation	New niche entered
Evolution of reproductive isolation	In isolation	In isolated niche
New distinct species after equilibration of new ranges		

The cat family.

...tes that grow on the ...and are the Cretan ...ecies of date palm. This is ...example of speciation by ...ographical isolation.

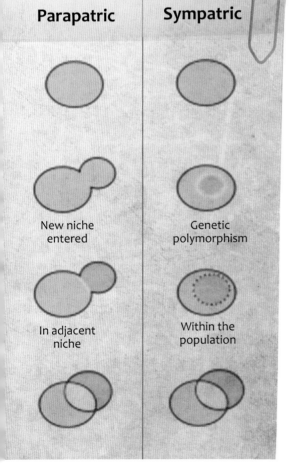

Parapatric	Sympatric
New niche entered	Genetic polymorphism
In adjacent niche	Within the population

The tick surviving on the body of a dog comes close to cospeciation except that the dog's body doesn't provide an environment long enough for the ticks to evolve.

Parapatric

In this type of process, there is no geographical barrier between the two species, but natural selection is the dominant factor, which causes only a particular type of species to survive and even if two species interbreed, their offspring is unable to survive.

Sympatric

This is a process in which two or more types of species evolve from the same ancestor without any geographical barrier and both types of species are able to survive.

With so much progress in science, there are ways by which we can induce speciation by animal husbandry, agriculture or using laboratory experiments.

Cospeciation

Cospeciation is the process where one population speciates in response with another and is a result of the associate's dependence on its host for its survival. In 1913, Fahrenholz termed cospeciation, however, in almost all instances, except those cases where the host is pathologically dependent on its associate, this principle is rarely, strictly adhered to. Deviations to the interpretation of Fahrenholz's rule are demonstrated by topological incongruence between the host and the associate's phylogenies.

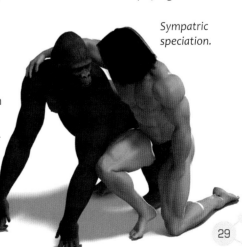

Sympatric speciation.

29

Genetics

The study of genetics includes variations, mutations, hereditary traits, genes and their structure, functioning, behaviour and distribution, and some other related topics. Epigenetics and population genetics are the subfields of genetics. Gregor Mendel, popularly known as the "father of genetics", studied genetics in the nineteenth century on pea plants.

What is genetics?

In genetics, we study genes and genetic code. Genes are the structures by which physical traits and characteristics are inherited.

In the human body, there are about 20,000 genes. A genetic code or a genome is somebody's genetic information. The presence of a particular type of gene is generally expressed with their function, which is transmitted to the offspring in the form of a particular sequence of amino acids. In common language, we can understand genetics as a science of the inheritance of different traits from the parents to their offspring. A baby with brunette parents will have black hair colour and a baby with blonde parents will have blonde hair. The shape of the nose and colour of the iris of a young one are likely to match their parent's. Thus, these are some of the many traits, which are inherited across generations.

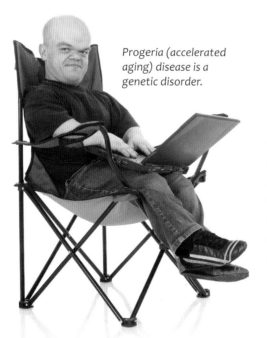

Progeria (accelerated aging) disease is a genetic disorder.

Genetic disorders

Diseases like colour blindness are hereditary and also known as genetic disorders. The types of genetic disorders are single-gene, autosomal dominant and recessive, X-linked dominant and recessive, Y-linked and mitochondrial. Colour blindness is a sex-linked disease. Colour blindness is the inability to differentiate between colours. This disease is mostly dominant in males. Females tend to be the carriers of this disease.

Genetics as a cure

Genetic research is the study of DNA and genes. These studies are used for the identification of genes or other factors, which are responsible for producing diseases. If we can find out the cause of a disease, it becomes easier to find a cure for it and also find ways to control the spread of that specific disease. Nearly, every disease we know today has some genes responsible for its occurrence. Some diseases have small and others have a large genetic contribution. The development of modern scientific research is in progress and in search of cures of diseases to enable us to lead a better life.

Advancements in genetics

There are many studies being carried out for more elaboration on the structure and organisation of genetic makeup, the regulation of gene expression and the study of variations and changes in genetic composition. Researches are occurring to elaborate fundamental biological problems using systems ranging from model organisms to the human body itself. Organisms chosen for experiments are those having short generations and hence, genetic manipulation becomes easy. For example, gut bacteria Escherichia coli, the plant Arabidopsis thaliana and baker's yeast (Saccharomyces cerevisiae) etc., are used for genetic manipulations. DNA manipulation is also currently possible in laboratories. Restriction enzymes are used for cutting DNA at a particular sequence and producing the required fragments of DNA. DNA fragments, by visualising through gel electrophoresis, can be separated. This is a vast field, where the possibility of many more researches still exists.

FUN FACT

Scientists love twins! An African tribe called Yoruba has the highest number of twin births, making them an interesting focus of genetic study.

Twins have DNA that is completely identical as they are formed by the same embryo.

UK scientists are seeking permission to genetically modify the human embryo.

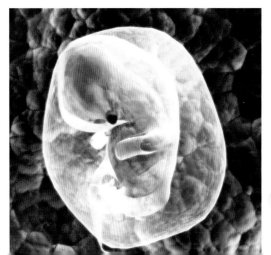

Cloning

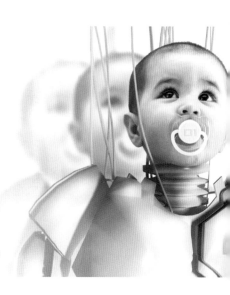

The process of creating a genetically identical copy of a cell or an organism is called cloning. Cloning happens all the time in nature. Prokaryotic organisms, such as bacteria and yeasts, create genetically identical duplicates of themselves using binary fission or budding. Eukaryotic organisms such as humans have cells that undergo mitosis. For example, the skin cells and the cells lining the gastrointestinal tract are clones.

Identical cells.

FUN FACT

In the 1880s, German Scientist Hans Driesch cloned the first animal ever. Using an embryo cell, he cloned a sea urchin.

Process of cloning

In biomedical research, cloning is broadly defined to mean the duplication of any kind of biological material for scientific study, such as a piece of DNA or an individual cell. For example, segments of DNA are replicated exponentially by a process known as polymerase chain reaction (PCR), a technique that is used widely in basic biological research. The type of cloning that is the focus of much ethical controversy involves the generation of cloned embryos, particularly those of humans. These are genetically identical to the organisms from which they are derived and could subsequently be used for research, therapeutic or reproductive purposes.

Cloning achievements

Reproductive cloning was originally conducted by artificial "twinning", or embryo splitting, which was first performed on a salamander embryo in the early 1900s by German embryologist Hans Spemann. Later, Spemann, who was awarded the Nobel Prize for Physiology or Medicine (1935) for his research on embryonic development, theorised another cloning procedure known as the nuclear transfer. This procedure was performed in 1952 by American scientists Robert W. Briggs and Thomas J. King, who used DNA from embryonic cells of the frog Rana pipiens to generate cloned tadpoles. In 1958, British biologist John Bertrand Gurdon successfully performed nuclear transfer using DNA from adult intestinal cells of the African clawed frogs (Xenopus laevis). Gurdon was awarded a share of the 2012 Nobel Prize in Physiology or Medicine for this breakthrough.

A computer generated image representing cloning.

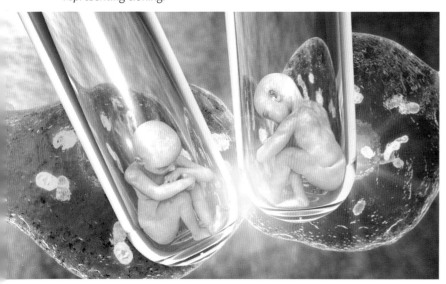

Twinning